WILD REACTIONS!

The Chemistry of Nature

Written by Joseph P. Cataliotti

WORLD BOOK

www.worldbook.com

Co-published by agreement between Shi Tu Hui and World Book, Inc.

Shi Tu Hui
Room 1807, Block 1,
#3 West Dawang Road
Chaoyang District, Beijing 100025
P.R. China

World Book, Inc.
180 North LaSalle Street
Suite 900
Chicago, Illinois 60601
USA

© 2026. All rights reserved. This volume may not be reproduced in whole or in part in any form without prior written permission from the publisher.

WORLD BOOK and the GLOBE DEVICE are registered trademarks or trademarks of World Book, Inc.

Library of Congress Control Number: 2025942238

Aha! Academy: Chemistry
ISBN: 978-0-7166-7346-0 (set, hardcover)

Wild Reactions! The Chemistry of Nature
ISBN: 978-0-7166-7351-4 (hard cover)
ISBN: 978-0-7166-7371-2 (e-book)
ISBN: 978-0-7166-7361-3 (soft cover)

Staff

Editorial

Vice President
Tom Evans

Senior Manager, New Content
Jeff De La Rosa

Associate Manager, New Content
William D. Adams

Senior Curriculum Designer
Caroline Davidson

Curriculum Designer
Mikayla Kightlinger

Proofreader
Nathalie Strassheim

Indexer
Nathaniel Lindstrom

Graphics and Design

Senior Visual
Communications Designer
Melanie Bender

Designer
Shannon Hagman

Written by Joseph P. Cataliotti

Designed by Starletta Polster

Acknowledgments

The publishers gratefully acknowledge the following sources for photography. All illustrations were prepared by WORLD BOOK unless otherwise noted.

Cover: critterbiz/Shutterstock; EAKARAT BUANOI/Shutterstock; Eric Isselee/Shutterstock; Gazi Mahmud Al Maruf/Shutterstock; MarBom/Shutterstock

© Mayo Clinic/Reuters/NBC News 33; Public Domain 7, 9; © Shutterstock 3, 4, 5, 6, 7, 8, 9, 10, 11, 12, 13, 14, 15, 16, 17, 18, 19, 20, 21, 22 , 23, 24, 25, 26, 27, 28, 29, 30, 31, 32, 33, 34, 35, 36, 37, 38, 39, 40, 41, 42, 43, 44, 45, 46, 47, 48

There is a glossary of terms on page 48. Terms defined in the glossary are in type that looks like *this* on their first appearance on any spread (two facing pages).

Contents

Introduction 4

1 Circles of life 6
Vital element: carbon 8
Carbon cycle 10
Anaerobic respiration 12
Aerobic respiration .14
Power from the sun 16
Vital element: nitrogen 18

2 Chemical communication 20
Secret plant chatter .22
Pheromones 24
Stinky chemistry 26

3 Wild chemistry 28
Crazy animal blood .30
Glowing in the dark 32
Venom and poison .34
Antifreeze frogs 36
Chitin 38
Spider silk 40
Honey bees 42

Experiments with leaves 44
Index 46
Glossary 48

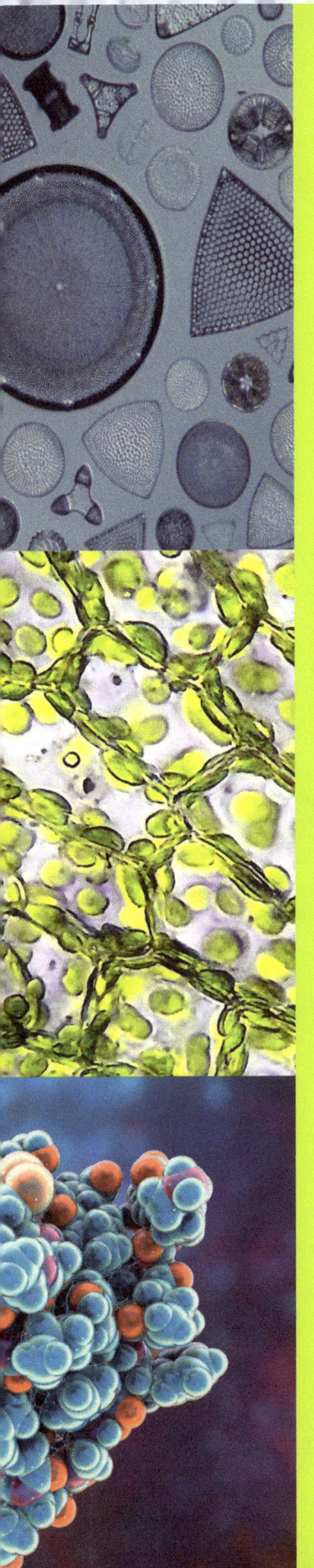

Introduction

Nature is full of wonder, from the tiny microbes in the soil to the timeless circle of life. However, nature is also full of mysteries. Have you ever wondered why animals like you breathe or how plants get their food?

Time for lunch!

Many wonders and mysteries can be explained through chemistry, the scientific study of the substances that make up everything and how they react with one another. By learning about chemistry, we can better understand the world around us and our part within it.

Keep reading to learn more about the chemistry of nature!

CIRCLES OF LIFE

You may not guess it, but carbon is the most important element to us living creatures. We'll talk more about carbon in the coming chapters!

The basic building blocks of all things in the world, including you, are miniscule atoms. Each of the chemical elements—*oxygen,* hydrogen, *carbon,* and all the others—is made of its own special atom.

When atoms come together, they form *molecules*. One of the most important molecules for life on Earth is *water*, or H_2O. A water molecule has two hydrogen atoms and one oxygen atom. You need water to live!

H_2O

Chemical *reactions* among different elements and molecules are the backbone of chemistry. In a chemical reaction, atoms come together to form a molecule or a molecule breaks apart, sometimes forming new molecules. Chemical reactions occur across nature and within our bodies, creating the *cycles* necessary for not only our survival but also that of all the other living things in the world.

The modern atomic theory of matter, which states that each chemical element is composed of its own kind of atoms, was first thought up by an English chemist named **John Dalton** over 200 years ago!

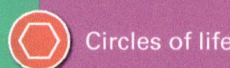

Circles of life

Vital element: carbon

STATS

Symbol
C

Atomic Number
6

Atomic Mass
12.0107

Discoverer
Known to ancients

Believe it or not, *atoms* are made up of even smaller particles! Each atom has a nucleus (core) made up of positively charged particles called protons and neutral particles called neutrons. Our friend *carbon* always has six protons and it usually has six neutrons.

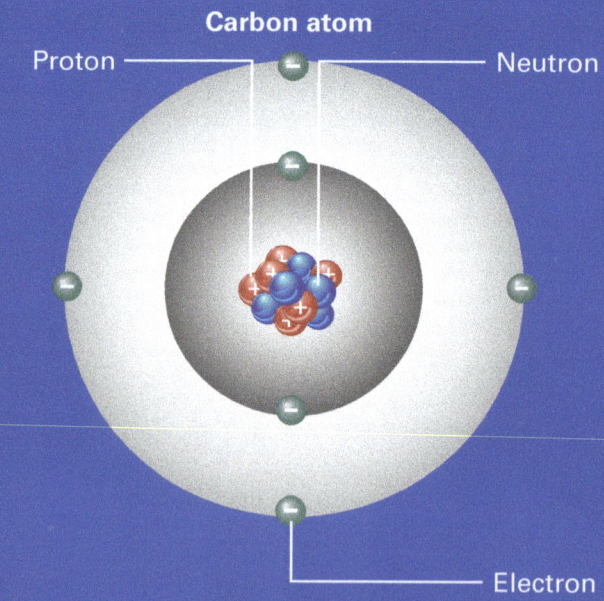

Carbon atom
Proton — Neutron — Electron

Even tinier particles, the negatively charged *electrons*, buzz around the nucleus. These electrons are responsible for the bonding between atoms.

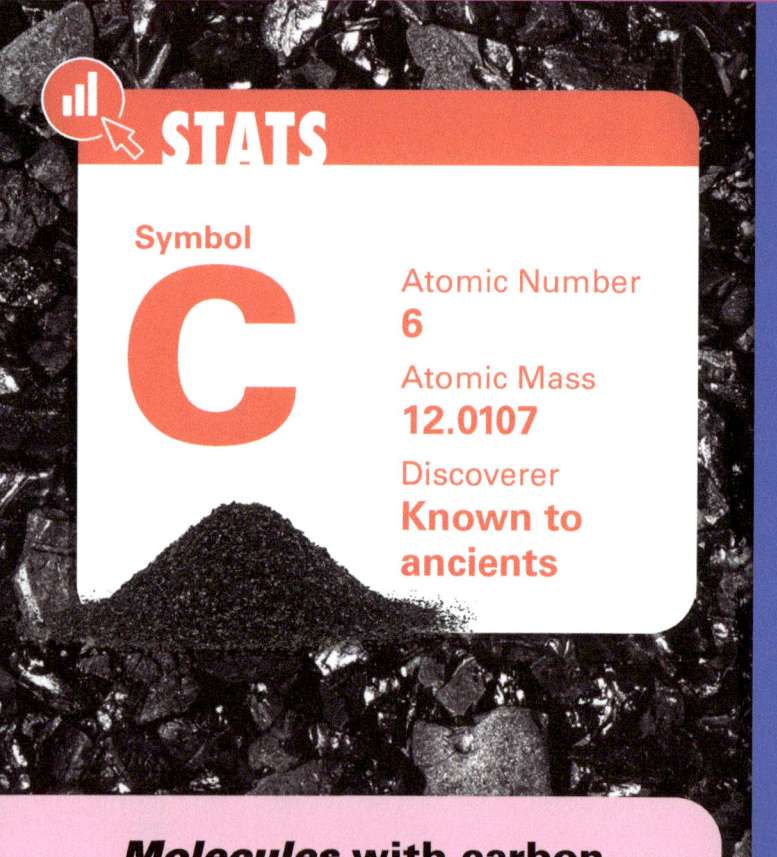

Molecules with carbon make up much of *you*. That's right, you're made of carbon, just like diamonds, graphite, and petroleum. Well, you're not *just* carbon—there are plenty of other elements inside of you, too.

The single most important element for us as life forms is carbon. Pure carbon can come together in large molecules to form beautiful diamonds or the graphite in your pencil.

Here's one carbon compound, pyruvate, that we'll talk about soon!

Carbon is great at bonding with other elements, forming large and complex molecules. There are more than 1 million known carbon *compounds*—the largest number of compounds formed by any element except hydrogen.

Carbon compounds make up the living tissues of all plants and animals. Organic chemistry—the study of compounds made by and derived from living things—is primarily the study of carbon compounds. Most *organic compound*s consist mainly of carbon combined with hydrogen, *nitrogen*, and *oxygen* in various combinations.

Circles of life

Carbon cycle

The total amount of *carbon* on Earth is constant. Carbon doesn't just disappear or pop into existence. Instead, the carbon *cycle* exchanges carbon among various locations and forms.

Where do plants get *their* carbon? Plants draw in carbon in the form of ***carbon dioxide*** (CO_2) gas from the air. The carbon becomes part of the plant through photosynthesis. Photosynthesis is a process in which plants, algae, and some other organisms use energy from sunlight to make food and the building blocks for growth.

Because you're presumably a human—a type of animal—you get your carbon from the food you eat. If you eat an animal, you get its carbon. That animal probably got its carbon by eating plants or other photosynthesizers. You could also just skip the line and eat plants directly.

But where does the carbon in the air come from? When living things die, the carbon inside them becomes trapped in the ground. There, certain bacteria may break down the once-living matter, releasing carbon back into the atmosphere as carbon dioxide.

Where does the carbon in your body come from? The process by which carbon circulates throughout the environment—including you—is called the carbon cycle.

The carbon cycle is a lot more complex than that. We didn't even talk about the vast amounts of carbon dissolved in the oceans, for example! But that overview should let you know the basics about *your* part in the carbon cycle.

Carbon is also in the fuel we burn to power our homes and cars. Over millions of years, once-living matter that remains in the ground can transform into these fossil fuels: coal, natural gas, and petroleum. When we burn fossil fuels for energy, the carbon that was captured by plants or algae or eaten by animals millions of years ago is returned to the atmosphere.

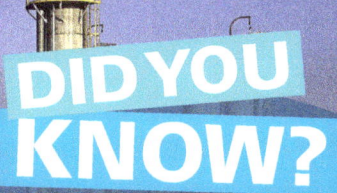

DID YOU KNOW?

Burning fossil fuels has raised the concentration of CO_2 in the atmosphere, driving climate change. However, the use of cleaner alternative energy sources is growing!

Circles of life

Anaerobic respiration

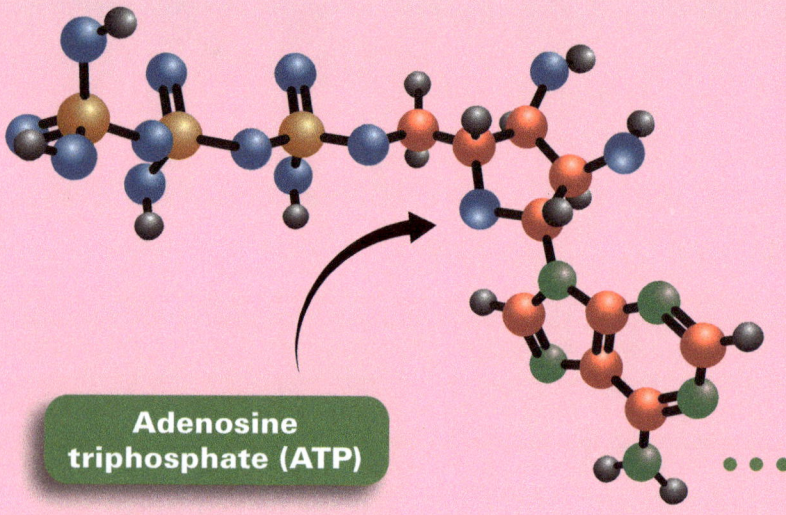

Adenosine triphosphate (ATP)

Anaerobic respiration is a type of **cellular respiration**. Cellular respiration is the process by which the **cells** in your body (and in the bodies of other animals) use **glucose**, or sugar, to make energy in the form of the **molecule** ATP.

The *oxygen* you breathe from the atmosphere is important to the cellular respiration happening right now in your very own cells. But, your body can keep making energy at a lower rate when oxygen in body tissues becomes more scarce, for example during a long run. This type of respiration without oxygen is called anaerobic respiration.

Have you ever run for so long your legs feel sore? That's because of anaerobic respiration.

Glycolysis is the first step in cellular respiration. In glycolysis, enzymes in your cells use one molecule of glucose, two molecules of NAD+, and two molecules of ATP to make two molecules of pyruvate, two molecules of NADH, and four molecules of ATP. This process is very complex, but as you can see, it produces a little bit of energy from sugar.

Nicotinamide-adenine-dinucleotide (NAD+)

If we animals don't have enough oxygen but still need to produce energy, a second process begins: lactic *acid* fermentation. In this chemical *reaction*, enzymes convert NADH and pyruvate from glycolysis into lactate and NAD+. That NAD+ is then recycled back into glycolysis to make more ATP! But it doesn't produce as much energy as aerobic respiration, and the cells have to get rid of the lactic acid buildup. This process is similar to the fermentation that makes the ethyl alcohol in alcoholic beverages.

Lactic acid

CAREER CORNER

Are you fascinated by these chemical reactions? Do you want to know more? Well, just your luck—you can become an organic chemist! These chemists study all sorts of *carbon*-based reactions and substances.

Circles of life

Aerobic respiration

Cellular respiration begins with glycolysis, in which enzymes in your *cells* use *glucose*, or sugar, and other *molecules* to make two molecules of pyruvate and several energy-storing molecules, including a net of two ATP molecules.

The next steps of cellular respiration require oxygen and are thus called *aerobic* respiration. Step two is the Krebs *cycle*. This process is complex, but it starts with pyruvate from glycolysis. A series of *proteins* gobble up the pyruvate, ripping off or plugging on new *atoms* to make new molecules. Ultimately, the Krebs cycle produces several important byproducts, including **carbon dioxide** and a few energy molecules.

Cellular Respiration

Glycolysis: Glucose → Pyruvate → NADN → ATP → Electron Transport → NADN → Krebs cycle → CO_2 → ATP → H_2O → ATP — Mitochondrion — Cell

CURIOUS CONNECTIONS

BIOLOGY The next two steps of aerobic respiration occur in the mitochondria (singular, mitochondrion). Mitochondria are one of many organelles, parts of the cell with a specialized function. Mitochondria are commonly called the powerhouses of the cell!

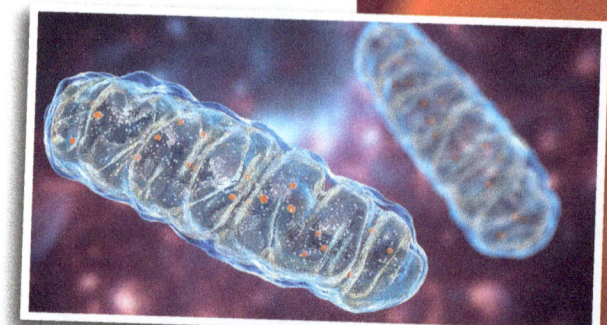

With just a bit of *oxygen* and *sugar*, aerobic respiration can create more than 30 molecules of ATP—far more than with anaerobic respiration alone!

The *electron* transport chain is the next step of aerobic respiration. Proteins in the membrane of the mitochondria snatch negatively charged electrons from those energy molecules made in the Krebs cycle. Special proteins use those electrons to pump positively charged hydrogen *atoms* into an area of the mitochondrion called the intermembrane space. Imagine these particles like water piling up behind a dam in a hydroelectric power operation.

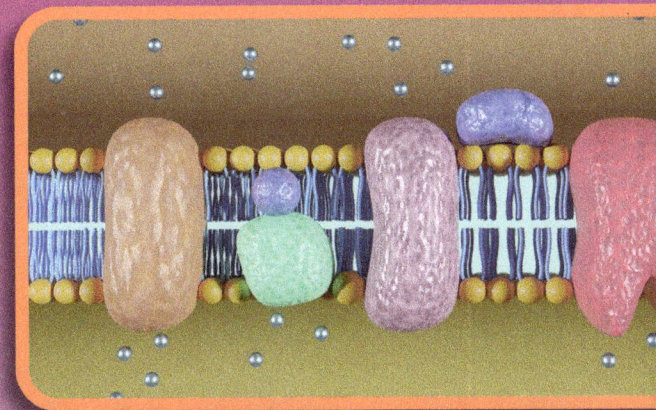

Hydrogen atoms escape the intermembrane space by passing through a rotating *protein* called ATP synthase, somewhat like water passing the turbine of a dam. ATP synthase uses the atom's passage to create ATP molecules—more than 30 for each glucose molecule that started glycolysis.

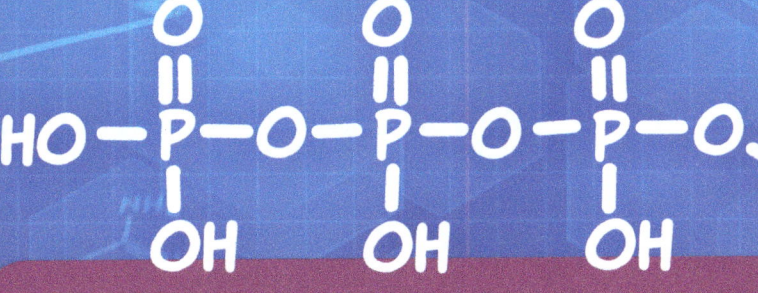

Cellular respiration occurs in your cells and the cells of every animal throughout the world. This is how we convert the food we eat into energy, using the air we breathe.

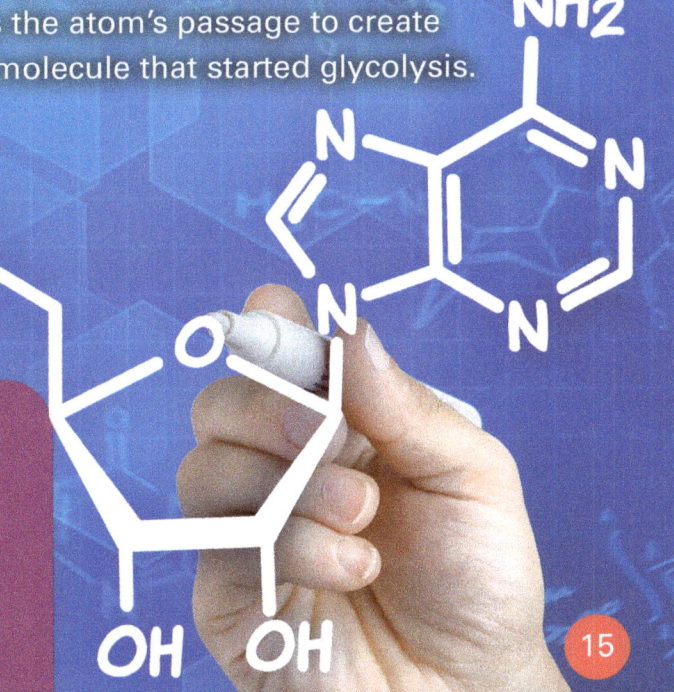

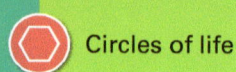
Circles of life

Power from the sun

The word photosynthesis means "putting together with light."

Green plants use sunlight to combine **carbon dioxide** and water to make food. This process converts light energy into the chemical energy of food.

Photosynthesis is the chief function of plant leaves. Plants absorb sunlight for photosynthesis with a green pigment called chlorophyll. Each food-making *cell* in a plant leaf contains chlorophyll in small bodies called chloroplasts.

Chlorophyll

Photosynthesis is an important chemical process in nature. It's how green plants, algae, and certain microorganisms make food with sunlight!

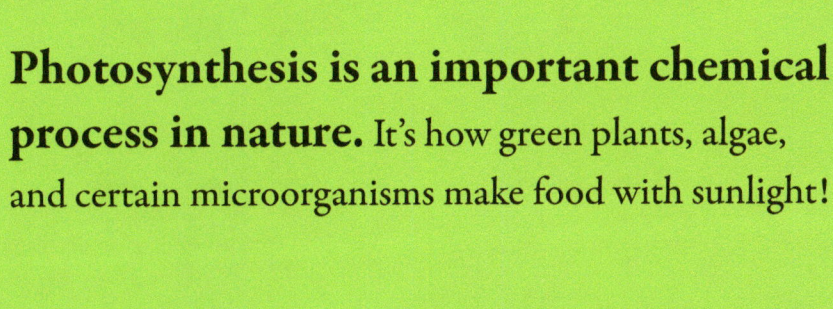

Inside chloroplasts, light energy causes water (H_2O) molecules to split, separating their hydrogen and *oxygen atoms*. In a series of complicated steps, the hydrogen combines with carbon dioxide to form a simple sugar. Oxygen from the water is given off in the process.

By combining sugar with *nitrogen*, sulfur, and phosphorus from the soil, green plants can make starch, fat, *protein*, vitamins, and other complex *compounds* essential for life. Photosynthesis provides the chemical energy needed to produce the food plants need.

DID YOU KNOW?

Plants aren't the only type of organism that can photosynthesize. Algae, such as seaweed, and cyanobacteria, which sometimes turn waters green, also get their energy from the sun.

Circles of life

Vital element: nitrogen

STATS

Symbol
N

Atomic Number
7

Atomic Mass
14.0067

Discoverer
Daniel Rutherford

***Nitrogen* is another important element for life.** All living things require nitrogen, but most organisms cannot use the nitrogen gas that makes up most of Earth's atmosphere. They need nitrogen that has combined with certain other elements to form *organic compounds*. The supply of this "fixed" nitrogen is limited, so living things have developed complex methods of recycling nitrogen.

Fortunately, there are tiny living things that have mastered the trick of splitting atmospheric nitrogen molecules and combining them with carbon, hydrogen, and oxygen to make new nitrogen-containing organic compounds. These bacteria can be found in soil, water, and in some plants, for example in the roots of legumes. This process is called nitrogen fixation.

Just as carbon circulates through the environment via the actions of living things and natural processes, so too does nitrogen. The circulation of nitrogen through the atmosphere, the soil and water, and the plants and animals of Earth is called the nitrogen *cycle*.

Ammonia

But nature recycles nitrogen, too! Certain bacteria and fungi produce ammonia from nitrogen compounds in once-living material and in body wastes excreted by animals. Plants absorb some of this ammonia and use it to make proteins and other substances essential to life. The rest of the ammonia is changed into molecules called nitrates by nitrifying bacteria. Plants absorb most of these nitrates and use them in the same way as ammonia.

How about you? Animals get nitrogen by eating those plants or by feeding on other animals that eat plants. Then the cycle continues!

TECH TIME

Human actions also affect the nitrogen cycle. Industry fixes vast quantities of nitrogen to produce fertilizer, much of which washes off farmland and into waterways, polluting the water. The combustion of certain fuels produces nitrogen compounds that pollute the air, too.

2
CHEMICAL COMMUNICATION

If you see a bear on the loose, you might call for help. But sound isn't the only way living things can communicate. Detecting and releasing chemicals is a major way to talk to the animals— and plants!

Perhaps one of the earliest senses developed by living things was the ability to detect chemicals. When you smell something wretched, your body is detecting its *molecules* and warning you to watch out! This is an important sense, especially if you don't like eating rotten food.

Animals, plants, and other forms of life have evolved ways to both release and detect chemicals in a way that is similar to other forms of communication. This process is called chemical signaling. Through chemical signaling, even plants can communicate to one another about oncoming danger!

Animals release chemicals called pheromones that can communicate all sorts of things to other animals. They can use pheromones to mark their territory or even attract mates. Scientists aren't quite sure if humans make use of pheromones, but many suspect we do!

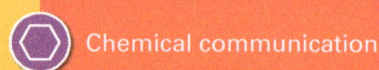
Chemical communication

Secret **plant chatter**

Plants can't communicate intentionally, the way people often do. Unlike you, plants don't have a brain. However, plants do emit chemical signals in response to changes in their environment.

Hello there!

For example, scientists have found that tomato plants emit a special type of chemical when munched on by pests. Nearby tomato plants can detect that chemical. Their *cells* quickly respond by triggering an immune *reaction*.

Believe it or not, plants can communicate! While they can't say "good morning," they can signal to one another using chemicals.

It's not just tomato plants that do this. Scientists have found plenty of other plants that release special chemicals to signal to other plants.

Plants may be able to detect whether the chemicals given off by other plants come from the same species or not. In addition, they might release just enough of the signal chemical to alert their friendly neighbors. They may curb their emissions to avoid tipping off farther plants—more likely to be a different species. In this way, plants may protect their buddies. There seems to be a whole realm of chatter among plants that we humans can't easily pick up on!

CAREER CORNER

Does chemical signaling in plants interest you? Consider yourself lucky: this field of biology has plenty of mysteries left to investigate. Study hard, and you can become a biologist and perhaps even solve those mysteries!

Chemical communication

Pheromones

Creatures that secrete pheromones range from single-celled organisms to rhesus monkeys and many other mammals.

Run!

Both males and females use pheromones to establish territories, warn of danger, and attract mates. For example, certain ants, mice, and snails release alarm pheromones when injured or threatened. The odor warns other members of the species to leave the area.

While animals howl, bark, and yelp, they can also unknowingly communicate through the release of signaling chemicals called pheromones.

Since 1959, chemists have developed synthetic pheromones. People use artificial female bug pheromones, for example, to bait and trap males of the same species. In another pest control method, called communication disruption, farmers spread their crops with fibers soaked in an insect pheromone. The odor of the pheromone prevents the male insects from finding females for mating. As an added bonus pheromones do not harm the environment, unlike conventional pesticides. Neat!

DID YOU KNOW?

Scientists have discovered some evidence that we humans produce pheromones that might signal to other humans. However, they are not quite sure yet if such signaling affects human behavior.

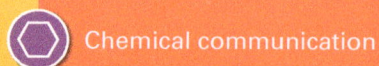 Chemical communication

Stinky chemistry

You can detect chemicals by breathing or sniffing the air. Many other animals can, too, sometimes much better than we humans. Dogs' sense of smell, for example, is as much as 100,000 times stronger than that of humans! See Spot sniff!

All sorts of animals use smells to detect tasty foods. Mosquitos, for example, find their prey (sometimes you!) by detecting exhaled *carbon dioxide* in a sense comparable to our own sense of smell.

Smell can enable you to tell the difference between rotten and fresh food before ever taking a bite. So next time you enjoy a snack, don't forget to thank your nose!

But how does your sense of smell work? We can detect smells if the air carries certain **molecules**. These molecules get caught by slimy, sticky mucus in your nose, then stimulate special smell-detecting **cells**. These cells send a nerve signal to your brain.

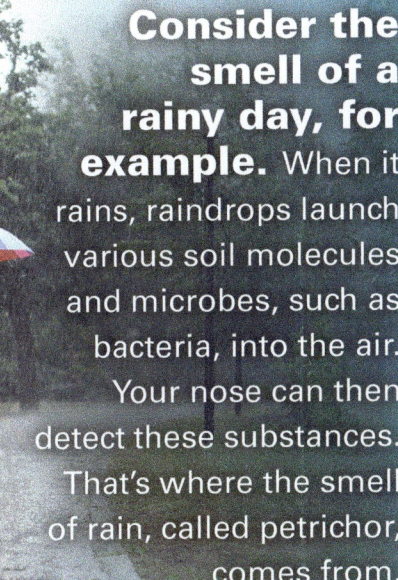

Consider the smell of a rainy day, for example. When it rains, raindrops launch various soil molecules and microbes, such as bacteria, into the air. Your nose can then detect these substances. That's where the smell of rain, called petrichor, comes from.

Scientists do not know exactly how we can distinguish smells from one another. One hypothesis is that it depends on how fast the smelly molecules stick to mucus and where in particular they attach to the smell cells in your nose. Another idea is that the molecules themselves trigger the smell cells differently. This mystery isn't completely solved!

3
WILD CHEMISTRY

Nature can show the bizarre side of chemistry. Blood isn't always red, some creatures can glow in the dark, and others can naturally produce poison or wondrously tough substances. These facts show how chemistry can make nature can appear almost magical!

You may be used to the sort of chemical *reactions* that occur in your everyday life, such as getting energy from sugar or your sense of smell, but chemical reactions in nature get much wilder.

Of course, the blue blood of octopuses, the poisonous skin of frogs, and the strength of spider silk are not magic. All of these can be explained by chemistry!

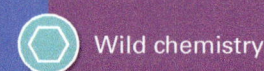

Wild chemistry

Crazy animal blood

Human blood includes several different types of *cells*. One type, the red blood cell, contains *molecules* of a *protein* called hemoglobin. Hemoglobin carries *oxygen* to cells with the help of iron *atoms*. Those iron atoms give your blood its red color!

While you have red blood, many animals have different colors. The octopus, for example, has blue blood. Instead of hemoglobin, octopuses have hemocyanin, a molecule with copper atoms. When bonded with oxygen, hemocyanin turns blue. Horseshoe crabs also have blue blood!

Your blood is a river of life that flows through your whole body, bringing oxygen and food to your cells. Many other animals have blood, but it's not always like ours!

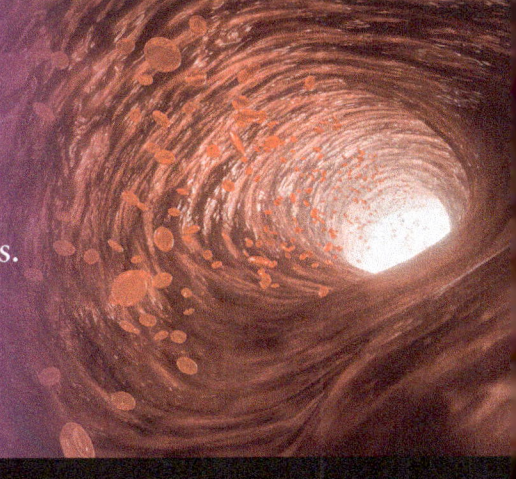

Some types of fish have clear blood, for example the ocellated icefish. The icy *waters* in which it lives have so much oxygen that the icefish doesn't need special molecules to bring oxygen to the cells that need it.

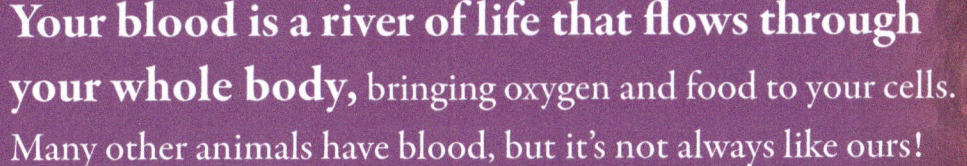

DID YOU KNOW?

Contrary to popular myth, human blood is never blue. Your veins, which carry your blood, look blue because of how light bounces off your skin. Blood that has little oxygen is, in fact, dark red, compared with the bright red of oxygenated blood.

Some species of skink have green blood! While these lizards have hemoglobin in their blood, they also have a green-colored molecule called biliverdin. Humans dispose of biliverdin in the body, but skinks do not, giving their blood a green color.

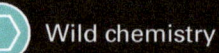
Wild chemistry

Glowing in the dark

The firefly, also known as the lightning bug, is a type of bioluminescent beetle. Fireflies get their glow from a chemical *reaction* between two types of *molecules*, luciferase and luciferin, and *oxygen*. When these substances react, light is produced.

Different bioluminescent species produce different types of bioluminescent molecules. This variation influences the color of their glow.

All sorts of animals are bioluminescent, meaning they can give off light. Most luminescent animals are found in the darkness of the deep ocean. For example, many squids are luminescent.

While fireflies may glow orange and yellow, other animals can glow red, green, or blue. For example, the sea firefly, a tiny crustacean only a few millimeters long, glows blue. Sea fireflies live in shallow *waters*. They're one of several bioluminescent organisms that can contribute a blue glow to waves at night.

🖱️ TECH TIME

Scientists have learned how to make other animals glow in the dark, too! By inserting a special bioluminescence gene into various animals—including cats—scientists have been able to make them glow in the dark. While fun, this experiment was done to see if a different gene, helpful for stopping infectious diseases, also took hold.

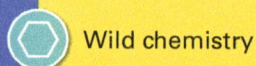

Wild chemistry

Venom and poison

Venom is a substance produced by many kinds of animals. Animals usually transmit venom by injection, generally by biting, stinging, or stabbing. They use venom to injure or kill prey, or to fight off attackers.

All sorts of creatures are venomous. Various snakes, spiders, scorpions, bugs, fish, and even some mammals produce venom!

What exactly is venom, though? Venom is a *toxin* made up of many different types of *molecules*, including specialized enzymes that can cause all sorts of trouble when they interact with your cells.

Venoms can cause harm in all sorts of ways. Substances in venom can cause numbness or paralysis or even stop the heart. Don't mess around with venomous critters!

Did you know there's a difference between venomous and poisonous? You should avoid both venomous and poisonous creatures though!

Venomous creatures can transmit their toxins by biting or stinging. Poisonous creatures deliver their toxins in nearly the opposite way—by being bitten or touched.

Few creatures are both poisonous and venomous. One is the blue-ringed octopus, which can deliver toxins by bite and also has toxins in its squishy flesh.

The poison dart frog, as its name suggests, is one poisonous creature. These frogs live in Central and South America. The skin of many species has glands that produce poisonous secretions to keep away predators.

CURIOUS CONNECTIONS

CUISINE — While being poisonous may be enough to deter normal predators, we humans aren't normal predators! A dish called *fugu*, popular in East Asia, is made from the carefully cleansed flesh of a poisonous pufferfish. Bon appétit!

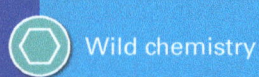

Antifreeze frogs

The wood frog of North America has a special evolutionary adaptation—it can survive being frozen. You and many other animals cannot. When animals freeze, ice crystals form inside their bodies and damage organs. Water also exits those organs, drying them out. This a good reminder to wear a winter coat when it's cold!

How do wood frogs survive being frozen?

The wood frogs that live in chilly Alaska produce and store large amounts of urea, **glucose**, and other special chemicals.

These chemicals prevent ice from forming inside the frog. They also have other benefits, such as providing fuel for the frog during winter inactivity. As the wood frog lies dormant, water also leaves its important organs, reducing the chances that damaging ice crystals will form there.

The long, bitterly cold winter descends on Alaska. The wood frog curls up in a hole in the ground. Its heart rate and breathing slow to a stop. But, the wood frog isn't dead! When spring comes, it gets up and keeps on hopping.

Two spring peepers, a species of frog found along the east coast of North America.

Other species of frogs can also survive freezing temperatures, including the gray tree frog and the spring peeper. Besides frogs, many different types of insects and fish can also survive bitter cold temperatures.

CAREER CORNER

Are you fascinated by all these funky creatures? Perhaps you should consider becoming a zoologist, a scientist who studies animals.

Wild chemistry

Chitin

The hard parts of such creepy-crawlies as spiders and bugs and such seafloor scuttlers as crabs and lobsters are made of chitin. (These animals all belong to a group called arthropods.) Chitin is both lightweight and strong. Chitinous critters can protect themselves from predators with tough shells or go after prey of their own with strong claws.

Like plant *cells*, fungus cells have cell walls to strengthen and protect them. But instead of cellulose, fungus cell walls are made of chitin.

What do fiddler crabs and fungi have in common? Chitin! This tough molecule provides support and protection to many kinds of living things.

Chitin is the basic building block of many creatures' shells. But, it takes many blocks to build a shell! Chitin is a polysaccharide, meaning it is made up of many interlocking sugar **molecules**. These molecules bond to make chains, which in turn form fibers.

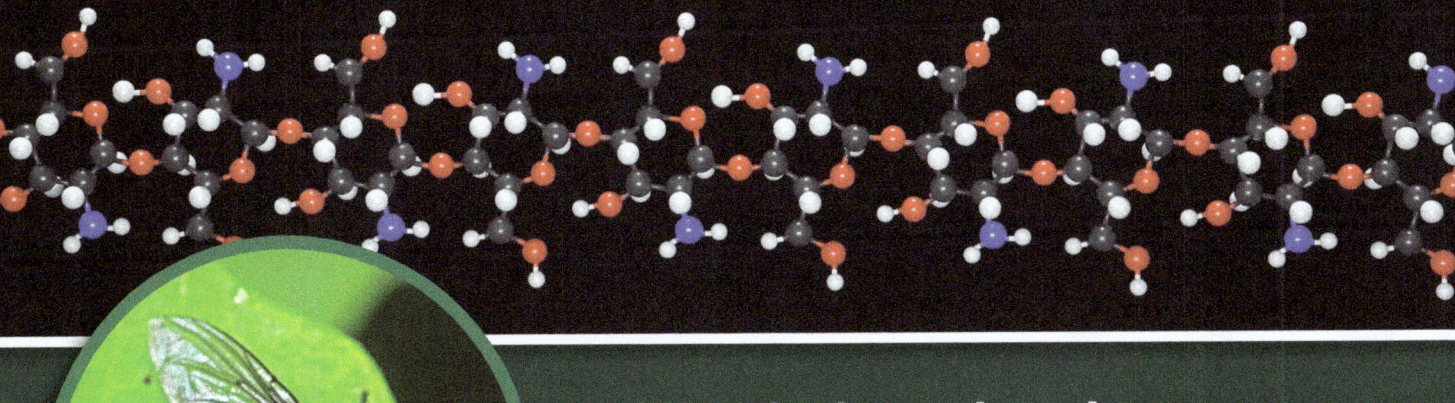

Chitin looks cool, too! Differences in the structures of fibrous units of chitin, the presence of other molecules or elements in the chain, and the presence of multiple layers can give chitinous hard parts all kinds of colors and sheens.

TECH TIME

In recent years, scientists have explored ways to make chitin artificially. This chitin can be used for a variety of purposes, such as encapsulating drugs or dressing wounds.

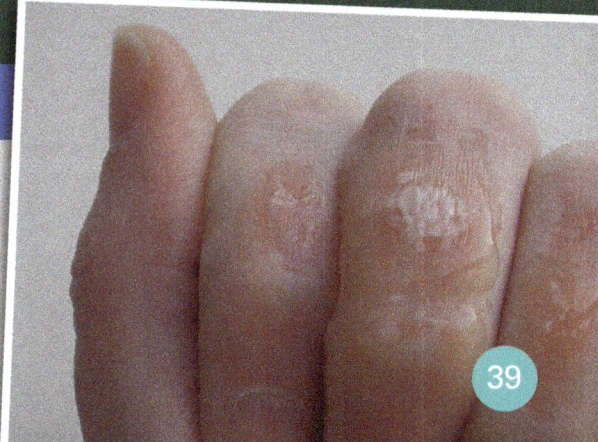

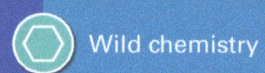 Wild chemistry

Spider silk

Spiders make their silk in special glands in their bodies. They then spin the silk with short, fingerlike structures called spinnerets on the rear of their abdomens.

Spider silk is primarily made of different types of *proteins*. Many repeating sequences of amino *acids* form the core of these protein *molecules*, with a specialized area of amino *acids* at either end.

Spider silk is a unique material. Not only is it stronger than steel, but some types are as stretchy as rubber!

Spiders use silk for many different things. They use it to construct their webs, which provide both a home and a net for catching tasty bugs. They can also use their silk to weave parachutes, as building material for tents, as food, and even to capture air for underwater breathing!

Spiders don't just produce one type of silk. The frame of spider webs, for example, is made of tough MA silk, named after the glands where it is produced—the major ampullate glands. In the flagelliform gland, spiders produce another type of silk that is highly elastic. Various spiders produce additional silk types! All the types of spider silk differ in their chemical structure.

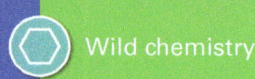 Wild chemistry

Honey bees

Honey bees build their homes using wax they make themselves. Bees will fight to guard their home from strangers. They can tell friend from foe by their smell.

When the threat to the hive is great, the guard bees give off a special pheromone. The scent of this pheromone, which smells like bananas, alerts other bees in the hive to come to the aid of the guards.

Flowers provide food for bees. The bees collect tiny grains of pollen and a sweet liquid called nectar from the blossoms they visit. They make honey from the nectar and use both honey and pollen as food.

Honey bees are one of the most impressive creatures. These buzzing insects live across the world and create some amazing chemicals—from honey to venom!

Honey is a mixture of many different *molecules*, chiefly such sugars as fructose, ***glucose***, and sucrose. There are also various amino ***acids*** and plenty of water. These ingredients make honey a healthy food for bees—and for us humans, bears, and many other creatures that eat honey.

While the honey bee produces delicious honey, bees can also produce a venom called apitoxin that they can inject into other creatures through their stingers. Apitoxin is a mix of many different molecules.

Bee venom has been used for thousands of years as a medicine for various ailments, including arthritis, because bee venom can reduce inflammation. Some researchers are investigating the use of bee venom in treating Alzheimer's disease.

Experiments with leaves

What you'll need:
- Fresh leaves from outside, however many you wish
- A clear bowl or glass for each leaf
- Water

Give it a try

1. Fill several clear bowls or glasses with water.
2. Collect leaves from outside. They can be any size or shape you can find, but make sure to include the stems. Don't pluck too many though!
3. Place your leaves inside the water containers, making sure they are submerged under the water. If a leaf floats back to the top, you can place a small rock or weight on the leaf to make sure it is submerged.
4. Now that you've prepared your containers, it's time for the fun part: testing different conditions. You'll need to think of different variables to test. Here are some ideas:
    - In the light
    - In the dark
    - In a cold place
    - In a room-temperature place
    - In a very warm place
5. Check your leaves every 30 minutes to see a key sign of photosynthesis: **oxygen** bubbles in the water and on the leaves!

Experts aren't the only ones who can do chemistry experiments—you can too! By collecting leaves, placing them in containers with *water,* and placing those containers in different conditions, you can observe different rates of photosynthesis with your very own eyes.

Try this next!

Your leaves have been through a tough test! Scientists carry out experiments by isolating and observing the effects of one specific variable, like whether or not a leaf is in light or shadow. What additional variables complicated your experiment? How might you isolate a specific variable to test its impact on photosynthesis?

QUESTION TIME!

In photosynthesis, plants convert light energy into food and a waste product, oxygen (which we humans then breathe in). What conditions were best for your leaves to photosynthesize? Why?

Index

A
acids, 9, 13-14
adenosine triphosphate (ATP), 12-15
aerobic respiration, 14-15
algae, 10, 17
amino acids, 40, 43
ammonia, 18-19
anaerobic respiration, 12-13
atoms, 6-8, 14-15, 17-18, 30

B
bacteria, 10, 17-19, 27
biliverdin, 31
bioluminescence, 32-33
blood, 28-31
blue-ringed octopuses, 35

C
carbon, 6, 8-11, 13
carbon dioxide, 10-11, 14, 16-17, 26
cats, 33
cells, 12-16, 22, 27, 30-31, 34, 38
cellular respiration, 12-15
chitin, 38-39
chlorophyll, 16
chloroplasts, 16-17
climate change, 11
communication between plants, 21-23
compounds, 9, 17-19
copper, 30
cycles, 7, 10-11, 14-15, 18-19

D
Dalton, John, 7
dogs, 26

E
electrons, 8, 14-15
enzymes, 13-14, 34

F
fireflies, 32-33
frogs, 29, 35-37
fugu, 35
fungi, 18, 38

G
glucose, 12-15, 36, 43
glycolysis, 13-15

H
hemocyanin, 30
hemoglobin, 30-31
honey bees, 42-43
horseshoe crabs, 30
hydrogen, 6, 9, 15, 17

I
iron, 30

K
Krebs cycle, 14-15

M
mitochondria, 14-15
molecules, 6-9, 12-15, 19, 21, 27, 30-32, 34, 38-40, 43
mosquitos, 26

N
neutrons, 8
nicotinamide-adenine-dinucleotide (NAD), 13-14
nitrogen, 9, 17-19

O
ocellated icefish, 31
octopuses, 29-30, 35
organic compounds, 9, 18
oxygen, 6, 9, 12-15, 17, 30-32, 44-45

P
petrichor, 27
pheromones, 21, 24-25, 42
phosphorus, 17
photosynthesis, 10, 16-17, 44-45
poison, 28-29, 34-35
poison dart frogs, 35
proteins, 14-15, 17, 19, 30-31, 40
protons, 8
pyruvate, 9, 13-14

R
reactions, 7, 13, 22, 28, 32
Rutherford, Daniel, 18

S
sea fireflies, 33
skinks, 31
smell, sense of, 21, 26-27, 42
spider silk, 29, 40-41
squids, 33
sulfur, 17
sunlight, 10, 16-17

T
tomato plants, 22
toxins, 34-35, 43

W
water, 6, 14, 16-19, 31, 33, 36-37, 43-45
wood frogs, 36-37

V
venom, 34-35, 43

Glossary

acid (AS ihd)—a type of molecule known by its special properties; it gives up a hydrogen atom in reactions

atom (AT uhm)—an incredibly tiny particle that makes up all things

carbon (KAHR buhn)—the most important element for life forms

carbon dioxide (KAHR buhn dy OK syd)—a gas that animals exhale as a waste product and plants use

cell (sehl)—the very small building block of all living things

cellular respiration (SEHL yuh luhr REHS puh RAY shuhn)—a series of chemical reactions that release energy from food

compound (KOM pownd)—a group of many of the same molecule

cycle (SY kuhl)—the circulation of elements and compounds throughout the environment

electron (ih LEHK tron)—a negatively charged particle that is smaller than the atom

glucose (GLOO kohs)—the chief source of energy for most living organisms

molecule (MOL uh kyool)—a group of joined atoms

nitrogen (NY truh juhn)—an important element that we need to make amino acids

organic compound (awr GAN ihk KOM pownd)—a compound that contains carbon atoms

oxygen (OK suh juhn)—an important element, found in air, that we need for respiration

protein (PROH teen)—a type of molecule made up of amino acids that is essential for life

reaction (ree AK shuhn)—a process by which one or more substances are converted into one or more different substances

toxin (TOK suhn)—a dangerous substance produces by a living organism

water (WAWT uhr)—a very important molecule made of two hydrogen atoms and one oxygen atom that all organisms use

www.ingramcontent.com/pod-product-compliance
Lightning Source LLC
Chambersburg PA
CBHW061256170426
43191CB00041B/2431